A COMPLIMENTARY REVIEW COPY, SPRING 1968

A HOW THEY LIVED BOOK

Flatboat Days On Frontier Rivers

BY JAMES McCAGUE
ILLUSTRATED BY VICTOR MAYS

ABOUT THE BOOK: This exciting documentary of early America brings to life for young readers the days when hearty men navigated clumsy flatboats down the Mississippi and Ohio Rivers to New Orleans in the late 1700's. How the flatboatmen lived and contributed to the early growth of the United States, what types of cargo and passengers they carried, and life in river towns is all vividly related here. This book is part of the *HOW THEY LIVED* series, designed to give young people a wider and more comprehensive view of American history and geography, and thus a deeper understanding and more lasting appreciation of their heritage.

Subject classification: Social Studies, American History
Sub-classification: Reading, Transportation, Opening of the Midwest

ABOUT THE AUTHOR: James McCague is well known in the book field as an adult novelist and historian. In his books he integrates in lively style the elements of history and transportation. He has recently turned his talents toward factual historical writing for children as well as adults. Born in Chicago and raised in a family of railroad men, he wrote Garrard's *When The Rails Ran West,* his first published juvenile. McGague was educated at Northwestern University and has lived in the Midwest most of his life. *Flatboat Days* is his third book for Garrard, following *Rails* and *Mississippi Steamboat Days.*

Reading Level: Grade 4   Interest Level: Grades 3–6
96 pages . . . 6⅞ x 9⅛   Publisher's Price: $2.39

Illustrated with old prints and engravings and 2-color drawings, full-color lithographed cover, reinforced binding, index, glossary

GARRARD PUBLISHING COMPANY

FLATBOAT DAYS ON FRONTIER RIVERS

were filled with the dangers of hostile Indians, murdering outlaws, and treacherous shoals on both the Mississippi and Ohio Rivers. Flatboats were a clumsy craft to navigate, but in the late 1700's and early 1800's, they were a vital part of river transportation.

Taking a load of cargo by flatboat to the busy port of New Orleans was a gamble. Pirates were rampant on the frontier rivers—and a vicious lot they were. Would the cargo sell for enough to make the long, hazardous trip worthwhile? Would the men survive the dangers along the way? If the flatboatmen succeeded in reaching their goal, they could enjoy a stay in bustling, colorful New Orleans before starting the long hike back to their homes.

The hardy folk who lived in those long-ago days come to life again in this fascinating book. Our nation's strength and growth are based on unique contributions of many kinds of people from all parts of the country. This book, part of a series called *How They Lived,* will give young people a deeper understanding and appreciation of American history as they see life in the past through the eyes of those who lived it.

Flatboat Days on Frontier Rivers

Flatboat Days
on Frontier Rivers

BY JAMES McCAGUE

ILLUSTRATED BY VICTOR MAYS

GARRARD PUBLISHING COMPANY
CHAMPAIGN, ILLINOIS

*To Tom, who might have been
a flatboatman in other days.*

Picture credits:

American Antiquarian Society: p. 19
American Museum of Natural History: p. 35
Boatmen's National Bank of St. Louis: p. 45
Brooklyn Museum: p. 22
Carnegie Library, Pittsburgh: p. 2, 17, 42
Cincinnati Historical Society: p. 12, back cover
City Art Museum of Saint Louis: p. 41, 47
Culver Pictures: p. 1
Historical Pictures Service: p. 87
I. N. Phelps Stokes Collection, New York Public Library: p. 71
Lilly Library, Indiana University: p. 90
Louisiana Historical Society, Courtesy of the Louisiana
    State Museum: p. 73
Louisiana State Library: p. 74, 75
Missouri Historical Society: p. 32, 44, 69, 88
Museum d'Histoire Naturelle, Le Havre, France: p. 40, 77
Museum of Science and Industry, Chicago: p. 15, 34, 79
New York Historical Society: p. 52, 53, 76
Picture Collection, New York Public Library: p. 24, 54, 80
Rare Book Division, New York Public Library: p. 5, 29, 38, 65
The American West by Lucius Beebe and Charles Clegg (New York:
    Charles Scribner's Sons, 1952): p. 120
Washington University Art Collection: p. 14

Endsheets: Painting by Felix Achille de St. Aulaire,
    Collection of Herman P. Dean

Contents

1. Parson Tucker

Three heavily laden flatboats floated down
the Ohio River one summer day in the year
1788. On board were several families from
Virginia, with all of their household goods.
They were settlers bound for new homes in the
region known as Kentucky, which stretched
along the south bank of the river.

On one of the boats was Parson Tucker, a
young minister who had come along to start
a church in the new settlement.

Dense forests covered both the riverbanks. In those early times few settlers lived there. But many Indian tribes did. Some of them were the enemies of all settlers. They knew from sad experience that white men always killed the deer and other game and took the best parts of the country for themselves. To them, the white men were spoilers of the land.

But the folk on the three flatboats were strangers in this great wilderness. Though they had high hopes, none of them knew what really lay ahead of them. Perhaps young Parson Tucker was wondering about that as he gazed out over the broad river.

Then all of a sudden, a cry was heard from the north bank. A man had run out of the forest there. He waved his arms and screamed at the flatboats. As they drew nearer, the folk saw that he was a white man. And he was crying for help.

Quickly some of the men seized the oars and rowed their clumsy craft toward shore. It never occurred to them to pass the poor fellow by.

Too late, they saw that they had been tricked.

No sooner had the first two boats touched the bank than a horde of yelling Indians burst out of the woods. A shower of arrows struck down many of the settlers. The rest, taken by surprise, had no chance to defend themselves.

Shrill war cries split the air. Stabbing and hacking with knives and tomahawks, the savage braves swarmed up over the flatboats' sides. They showed no mercy. In a few minutes every person on both boats was killed.

The third flatboat, lagging a little way behind the others, had not yet reached the shore. Some of the men on board tried to row away. Others had time to snatch up their flintlock rifles as the Indians came splashing through the shallow water to attack them too.

They fired one hasty volley. Then, using the long rifles as clubs, they beat the braves back. But there were too many Indians. They kept on attacking. One by one, the white men went down in fierce, hand-to-hand fighting. At last the flatboat drifted out into deep water again.

Now only one of the men on board was left alive. It was Parson Tucker. He was bleeding from many wounds. And the battle was not yet over.

Several braves dragged a canoe from its hiding place among some reeds on the river-bank. Leaping into it, they paddled swiftly after the drifting flatboat.

The women on the boat were as brave and hardy as their husbands had been.

One woman picked up an empty rifle lying on the deck. She tore the powder horn and bullet pouch from a dead man's body. Quickly she poured a big charge of gunpowder down the rifle barrel. With the long ramrod she rammed a bullet down on top of it. Then she rammed in a patch of greased cloth to hold the bullet in place.

But all this took time. The speedy canoe was drawing closer. Coolly the woman cocked the rifle and handed it to Parson Tucker. In

spite of his wounds, he stood up and took careful aim.

Bang! A brave yelled in pain and fell out of the canoe.

Other women were loading rifles also. They passed them to Parson Tucker, each in turn. And he was a good shot. Every bullet hit its mark. Soon only a few Indians were left alive in the canoe. They had had enough. Turning away, they paddled back to shore as fast as they could go.

Thankfully, some of the women bandaged the young preacher's wounds. The rest took hold of the long, heavy oars and rowed the flatboat

The banks of the Ohio River were dotted with
new settlements, among them Cincinnati, seen in
this early print.

down the river as best they could. After a
while they managed to reach Limestone, a
small settlement on the Kentucky shore. Then
at last they were safe. But Parson Tucker was
so badly hurt that he died a few days later.

All that we know of this sad event comes
from a story written by a man named James
Finley. As it happened, Finley traveled down
the Ohio with another group of flatboats only
a few weeks later.

He told of his own party's narrow escape,
"A long and desperate effort was made to get
some of the boats to land by a white man who

feigned to be in great distress. . . ." But the leaders of Finley's party had been warned about this sort of thing and would not stop.

The trick was often played by white outlaws who had run away and joined the Indians. No one knows how many poor flatboat people they murdered and robbed.

James Finley's brief tale does not tell us what became of the widows whose husbands had been killed. Perhaps some of them made their way back to Virginia. But no doubt many stayed on and made homes for themselves in the wild Kentucky country. They were not the kind of people who gave up easily.

In spite of the dangers and the hardships, more and more such settlers came floating down the Ohio River every year. America was a young, growing nation. Americans were pushing westward, seeking new land and new opportunities in the distant wilderness.

The great, broad river was a natural roadway for them to follow. And nothing could stop them.

Pioneers, led by Daniel Boone, are shown crossing
the Cumberland Gap in this painting by Bingham.

2. Moving West

People like the settlers with Parson Tucker were called emigrants. Many of them had come a long way before they ever reached the Ohio River.

They had trudged over rough, stony roads through the Allegheny Mountains with their belongings piled in wagons or on the backs of pack horses. Boys and girls had walked beside their mothers and fathers. Most families had driven their cows, pigs, and other farm animals right along with them.

Some of these people came from eastern Pennsylvania. Some came from Maryland, Virginia, or other states along the shores of the Atlantic Ocean. Nearly all of them headed for the town of Pittsburgh, in western Pennsylvania.

There, among the foothills of the mountains, two big rivers meet to form the Ohio River. One is the Allegheny, flowing down from the northeast. The other, the Monongahela, flows from the south. At the forks where they come together stands Pittsburgh.

Today Pittsburgh is one of America's greatest cities. Even in those long-ago times, it was an important town. Around 1800 a traveler named William Irish counted more than 700 houses there. Most of the people who lived in these houses, he wrote, were either innkeepers or boatbuilders.

It was no wonder. The first thing that weary emigrants looked for when they got to town was a place to stay. Then they hurried out to see about buying a flatboat.

We can still read some of the boatbuilders' advertisements in old copies of the town's first newspaper, the *Pittsburgh Gazette*. One described his flatboats as "comfortable family boats, well boarded up the sides and roofed to within seven or eight feet of the bow." He also quoted his price: one dollar per foot of length.

A flatboat usually was about 30 or 40 feet long and about 12 feet wide. But even $30 was a big sum of money in those days. Many poor folk did not have that much to spend. So they would have to find other families to share the cost of a flatboat.

The boatyards stretched for several miles along the banks of the Allegheny and the Monongahela Rivers. They were noisy, bustling places.

This Pittsburgh boatyard provided many of the boats that took settlers to their new homes on the Ohio.

Brawny workmen were busy sawing big logs into planks. Other men used adzes to hew out square beams for flatboat frames. An adz was a tool something like a combination of an ax and a garden hoe with a sharp blade. Chips flew in all directions as the men worked. A smell of sawdust and shavings filled the air.

At the river edge, hammers clattered away. The thick planks were fastened to the boat frames with stout wooden pegs instead of nails. Seams between the planks were stuffed with strands of tarred rope, called oakum, to make them watertight. When the boat was finished, she was pushed down long, slanting timbers into the water.

Not all flatboats were exactly alike. But they all looked like big wooden boxes about four or five feet deep. The sides rose straight up from the flat bottoms. Both bow and stern were perfectly square. But the under part of the bow usually slanted upward a bit, like the front of a sled, so that the boat could go through the water a little more easily.

A few very big flatboats might have pointed bows and sterns. They were called arks. Some small ones, called scows or sheds, had rude cabins in the middle. Allegheny skiffs had

Charles Lesueur, a French artist, drew these flatboats
while traveling down the Ohio River.

larger, flat-roofed houses which occupied most
of the deck.

The commonest kind of flatboat was known
as the Kentucky boat. A low roof covered
most of her length, except for a short space
at the bow. This roof usually slanted down-
ward slightly on both sides.

All flatboats were steered with a long, heavy
oar trailing astern.

The boat could also be rowed by means of
two big oars at the bow. These were called
gouge oars. They must have looked like a pair
of horns sticking out, for Kentucky boats were
often called "broadhorns."

This, then, was the family home—maybe the home of more than one family—for the long trip down the Ohio River. She was not a pretty craft, but she was roomy. And if the workmen had done their jobs well, she was good and sturdy.

Under the low roof were stowed all of the things the emigrants would need. Each family was sure to have brought a plow, some pots and kettles, an ax, a grindstone, and maybe a spinning wheel. There were warm blankets and quilts, several sides of bacon, and a few bags of flour or cornmeal.

There was time for fun as well as chores on the long trip downriver.

Of course the men had their rifles, a supply of gunpowder, and some bars of lead to be melted down and made into bullets. Very likely there was a jug of whiskey too. The settlers who lived by the Monongahela River were famous for the whiskey they made.

In whatever space was left, the families would live and sleep and eat their meals. The women cooked over a fire in a box full of sand, with a stovepipe sticking up through the roof to carry off the smoke. We must not forget the animals. They went along too.

One man who traveled down the Ohio in 1815 was reminded of Noah's Ark by some of the flatboats he saw. In a book he wrote, he told of ". . . old and young, servants, cattle, hogs, sheep, fowls, and animals of all kinds . . . all embarked and floating down on the same bottom. . . ."

But this same man, whose name was Timothy Flint, told of seeing dead men floating past too. And, he wrote, the wreckage of flatboats was often strewn along the banks of "this wicked river." So we can guess that some of the emigrants knew little about handling boats and often got into trouble.

Nevertheless, like Noah and his family in

the Bible, most of them finally came safely to land.

Many settled along the south side of the Ohio River, in Kentucky. One small settlement that started there in 1778 became the city of Louisville. Another city, Cincinnati, grew up around a log fort built in 1788 in what is now the state of Ohio.

Gradually, the hostile Indians were driven off. More and more towns and villages and farms sprang up. Soon folk began to settle even farther west, in the territories of Indiana and Illinois.

Often they simply ran their flatboats onto the shore and went on living in them while they chopped down trees, plowed the earth, and planted crops. Then they took the boats apart and used the planks and beams in the cabins they built. They were no longer flatboat folk; they were farmers.

But many of them soon found that their flatboat days were not over, after all.

These backwoods settlers had to fell and burn trees to clear off their land for planting crops. Painting by George Harvey.

3. A Cargo for New Orleans

To a lively lad growing up on a farm near the Ohio River, harvest time was an exciting time indeed. It meant more than just gathering the crops that had been growing all summer. It meant a voyage to New Orleans.

And every young fellow with a drop of red blood in his veins hoped he would be lucky enough to make the trip.

New Orleans was far away in Louisiana, down the Ohio and the Mississippi Rivers. Until 1803 it was a foreign city, besides. The French had settled it first, many years earlier. Then Spain owned it for a long time, along with most of the vast land that lay west of the Mississippi.

Its location on the Gulf of Mexico made it the only seaport in all the middle part of America. That was why the commerce of the whole broad Ohio Valley flowed down to New Orleans. And it flowed along the two great rivers, the Mississippi and the Ohio.

Trappers and hunters from the forests carried their furs there in big canoes that were called pirogues, or in large skiffs that they called bateaus. Merchants and traders took the goods they wanted to sell to New Orleans. From there, they could be shipped by sea to large cities along the east coast, or to Europe. Farmers, when the time came to market their crops, had to go to New Orleans too.

As harvest time drew near each year, the settlers at every town and landing place along the Ohio River began to get their flatboats ready.

Most of the river towns had boatyards now. But many of the thrifty farmers had learned how to save money by building their own boats. Sometimes a group of farmers in a neighborhood got together to build a boat.

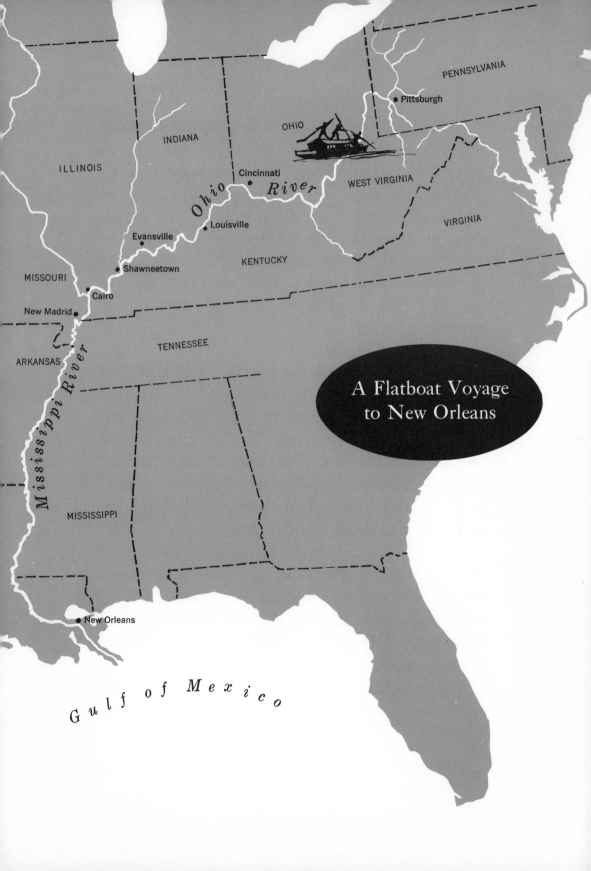

PENNSYLVANIA

• Pittsburgh

OHIO

INDIANA

ILLINOIS

Ohio   River

Cincinnati

WEST VIRGINIA

VIRGINIA

• Louisville

Evansville

KENTUCKY

MISSOURI

• Shawneetown

• Cairo

New Madrid

TENNESSEE

ARKANSAS

Mississippi River

MISSISSIPPI

A Flatboat Voyage
to New Orleans

• New Orleans

Gulf   of   Mexico

All summer long, whenever they could spare time from their farm chores, they worked away with axes, adzes, and hammers. Slowly the flatboat took shape on some dry sandbar at the river edge. As they worked, the people thought about a name for her.

A boat might be named after some member of a farmer's family, like *Betsy*, *Polly*, or *George*. One boat we know of was named *Brother and Sister*. Some people chose fancier names like *Liberty* or *Orleans Packet*. Or a hopeful, good-luck name might be chosen, like *Good Return* or *Swift Safety*.

Autumn usually brought rainy weather. The rain made the river rise, flooding the sandbar and setting the heavy flatboat afloat. Then at last, as October days grew nippy with frost and the red and yellow leaves fell from the trees, it was time to load her.

Barrels of flour ground at the local mill were rolled down the riverbank and stowed on board. Other barrels were packed with pork, freshly butchered and preserved with salt. Smoked hams and slabs of bacon were hung under the flatboat roof.

There were barrels of apples, butter, tallow, cheese, and many other things. The rich, black

28

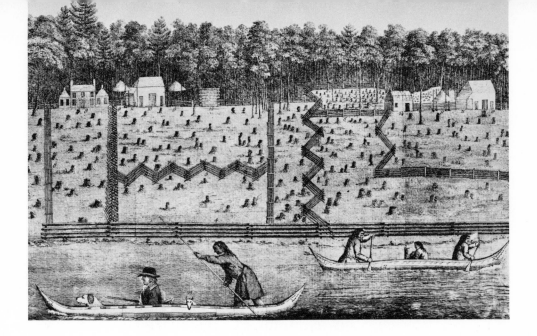

Indians and a settler pass by the crude buildings and
newly-cleared fields of a backwoods farm.

earth along the Ohio River grew all sorts of
fine crops.

Kentucky farmers often had tobacco to ship.
Some of them had learned to make whiskey
out of the grain they raised. So that too was
often shipped on the Kentucky boats. Farmers
in Ohio and Indiana sent along bags of shelled
corn and of potatoes, and timbers of pine or
cherry wood from the nearby forests.

All of these cargoes could be sold at New
Orleans. But New Orleans was so far away
that no one could possibly know what price a
cargo would bring by the time it arrived. A
flatboat voyage was a kind of gamble. Would

the cargo sell for enough to make the trip worthwhile? Would the men survive the danger along the way?

Outlaws still lurked in the wild country farther west. Rocks and shoals, rapids and swift river currents threatened the boats along the way. Sunken logs with jagged limbs, called snags, could wreck even the stoutest flatboat.

However, the captain of the flatboat was usually an experienced riverman. The crew was generally a couple of husky farm boys from the neighborhood. And, whenever it was possible, several flatboats would travel together. That way, their crews could help each other in case of trouble.

Unfortunately, no writer has left us a first-hand report of the start of a flatboat voyage. But we know that it must have been an important event. Every family sending cargo surely came down to the riverbank to see her off, and to wish the voyagers good luck.

No doubt a prayer was said for their safe return. No doubt the younger boys and girls ran about in great excitement. The sturdy lads chosen for the crews probably tried to look very brave as they told the girls good-bye.

The boys and men wore their ordinary working clothes: baggy shirts of flannel or calico and linsey-woolsey coats and trousers. Linsey-woolsey was a rough homespun cloth made of wool mixed with linen or cotton. They wore broad-brimmed hats or stocking caps.

Each man carried his budget, a small bag with a few personal belongings, wrapped in a blanket or buffalo robe.

The good-byes did not take long. With stout poles the flatboatmen pushed their boats away from the bank. Each captain took hold of his long steering oar. The men ran out the heavy gouge oars and began to row. Slowly the clumsy craft moved out toward the middle of the river.

The current rippled about them. Now they

moved a little faster. Soon they swung around a bend in the river. Homes and families were left behind. The flatboatmen were on their own.

If all went well, it would take them about five or six weeks to reach New Orleans. At least three or four more months would pass before they came back home again. But every man was looking forward to the voyage.

It certainly would beat plowing a cornfield, or hoeing a potato patch or grubbing stumps out of the ground or chopping wood all day. Life on a backwoods farm was rough and harsh. Most of the time it meant nothing but dull, hard work from morning until night.

Going down to New Orleans on a flatboat offered these simple farm boys a chance to have some fun. It would give them a taste of the great, wide world away from home. And they meant to make the most of it.

A minister named Robert Baird, who met many of the flatboatmen in his travels along the Ohio, has given us a hint of how they felt. "Even decent, quiet deacons at home would throw aside religion and peace when they embarked on their annual trip downriver," he wrote rather sadly.

They were off on a great adventure.

4. Floating Down the River

John James Audubon got on a flatboat at Cincinnati, Ohio, one fine October day in 1820. He was not really a flatboatman. He was an artist who wanted to travel down the river, painting pictures of all the wild birds to be seen along the way.

But he kept a daily journal telling about his trip. And from it we learn a great many things about flatboatmen and how they lived.

Audubon was on one of two boats that were traveling together. He described one of the captains, Jacob Aumack, as a good, strong young man. He was careful in handling his flatboat, "yet brave and accustomed to hardships." The captain of the other boat was named Loveless. He was "a good-natured, rough fellow . . . playful and fond of jokes."

A man named Shaw owned most of the cargo in the two flatboats. He had come along too. But Audubon did not like him very well. He thought that Shaw was stingy and selfish.

Four men made up the crews of the flatboats.

One, Ned Kelly, was "a wag of 21, stout, well made, handsome if clean." Evidently he was often dirty. Ned also bragged a lot, and the other men made fun of him. But, wrote

John James Audubon posed for this painting by his sons many years after his flatboat trip.

Audubon, "he sings, dances, and feels always happy."

Two others were men from Pennsylvania who worked hard, minded their own business and talked very little. The fourth man, named Joe Seeg, was a lazy, stupid young fellow. Audubon noted that he was "fond of grog."

All in all, these men probably were like most flatboatmen. They had their faults, but they were tough and hardy, as flatboatmen had to be. Audubon soon saw proof of that. The second night after leaving Cincinnati, both boats ran aground.

It was a raw, chilly night with a north wind

blowing. But the poor men had to scramble overboard. Splashing and stumbling over the slippery river bottom, they pushed and tugged at the heavy boats. Sometimes they were waist-deep in the icy water. But the boats floated free at last.

Luckily, neither one was damaged. The men climbed back on board. They were used to things like that. "Such life is well-intended to drill men gradually to hardships, to go to sleep with wet, muddy clothing on a buffalo skin stretched on a board," wrote Audubon later.

After that, Aumack and Loveless no longer tried to travel at night. They pulled into shore

These flatboatmen have tied up for the night near a settlement on the Mississippi River.

each evening and tied up to the bank until next morning, as most flatboatmen did.

Even in daylight it was not easy to keep from running aground. An awkward, heavily loaded flatboat was hard to manage. Just pushing and pulling the long steering oar was hard work. Sometimes the steersman had to yell for his crew to take the gouge oars and row the boat away from a snag or a sandbar.

Once in a while, when the river swung around a sharp bend, the strong current drove the boat in toward the bank. No matter how hard the crew tugged at the oars, they could not keep her clear.

Then they had to hurry and launch the small rowboat, or skiff, that was carried on board. One man jumped into it with the end of a long, stout rope. He rowed for the opposite bank as hard as he could. Quickly he tied the end of the rope to a rock or a tree.

Another man took several turns of the rope around a strong check post built into the flatboat. By bracing himself and letting the rope out very slowly, he made it act like a brake. This slowed down the boat and kept her in the middle of the river until she floated safely around the bend.

Then the man with the skiff had to untie the rope and row hard to catch up.

When hard work like this made a man hungry, he simply cooked his own meal and ate it whenever he had the chance. The crew seldom ate together, and there was no regular cook.

Audubon explained that he usually cleaned and roasted a duck or a partridge he had shot for himself. But some of the men did not take so much trouble. He wrote: "Others preferring bacon would cut a slice from the side that hung by the chimney, and chew that raw with a hard biscuit."

The only way to get inside this flatboat's cabin was down the hatch! Dinner cooks in the fireplace.

It was a rude, rough life, no doubt about that. Yet it was not all hardships. Sometimes the river ran along in calm, straight stretches. Then the days could be quite lazy and easygoing.

Great numbers of wild animals and birds lived in the forests on both sides of the Ohio River. This was a hunter's paradise, in fact. And evidently the flatboatmen liked to hunt. Audubon told how they once came upon a deer swimming in the river.

They chased him in their skiff, but "a canoe with two Indiana men had the advantage of us, and caught it as I rose to shoot it."

Another time they saw a bear on shore.

40

They chased him too, but he escaped. They often shot partridges, swans, squirrels, and wild turkeys. Flatboatmen were never in much of a hurry. They seemed to stop and go ashore to hunt whenever they felt like it.

In 1820 when Audubon made his trip, all sorts of people were floating down the Ohio on all sorts of craft. Some poor or shiftless folk had nothing but flimsy rafts made of logs bound together with ropes. A few venturesome fellows even drifted along in frail rowboats.

"Gayly we were overtaken by a skiff containing a couple of gentle young men bound to New Orleans," wrote Audubon one autumn

River traffic in 1820 included huge rafts which were poled downriver and sold in New Orleans as lumber.

day. "They had mattresses, trunks, a gun and provisions. . . ."

Other flatboats—Kentucky boats, Allegheny skiffs, arks—were seen just about every day. Long, narrow boats called keelboats went past occasionally.

The flatboatmen often had business to take care of on shore. Audubon told how they landed near Evansville, Indiana, one day. A man who lived there owed some money to Mr. Aumack, and the captain wanted to collect it.

Among these river folk trading was much more common than buying and selling. Mr.

A flatboat drifts lazily downriver as the crew of a passing keelboat strain at their poles to move the boat against the current.

Aumack didn't get his money. Instead, "he brought on board only a French double barrel gun and a gold watch." So we may suppose the debt was paid.

Sometimes the sights along the river were very lovely. As an artist, Audubon noticed beauty. We find this entry in his journal:

"The weather fair this morning, the thermometer down at 30. The sun rose beautiful and reflected through the trees on the placid stream like a column of lively fire. The frost was heavy on the decks and when the sun shone on it, it looked beautiful beyond expression."

Later that same day he wrote: "We floated tolerably well, the river here being contracted by large sandbars. . . ."

It was November now, and the flatboats had come a long way. In fact, they were drawing very near to the most difficult and dangerous stretch of the whole Ohio River. At the head of this stretch stood Shawneetown, on the Illinois shore. And in those days, Shawneetown was one of the busiest of all the river towns.

No flatboatman ever passed by there without stopping for a while.

5. Shawneetown

When they rowed their flatboats in toward
the Shawneetown landing, the crews were likely
to find a big crowd of other boats already there.

Sometimes there was no more room for boats
along the shore. Then each boat was just tied
fast to another one, until they all formed a
huge, floating mass that stuck far out into the
river. A man going ashore from his flatboat
might have to walk across six or seven other
boats before he stepped on dry land.

As he looked around, it seemed that he was
already in a town. It was a town of boats.

44

There, close by, was a small flatboat with a house built on its deck. A calico flag fluttered from a pole on its front end. The flag was a sign showing that this was a store boat. If business was not good, the storekeeper himself might be standing out on deck, tooting on a tin horn to attract customers.

The chances were, though, that Shawneetown housewives in homespun dresses and calico sunbonnets already had hurried on board.

Inside the store boat were shelves and bins full of supplies for sale. There were shirts, pantaloons, hats, coats, and rolls of cloth. There were papers of pins and needles, spools of

The peddler with his flatboat filled with notions and tinware was a welcome visitor at all settlements.

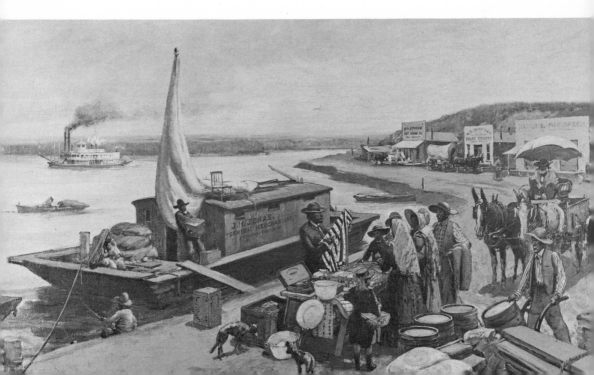

thread, knives, and scissors. From hooks on the walls and ceiling hung iron kettles, frying pans, tin pots, and other hardware.

There might be a bag of coffee, a box of tea, a few jars full of precious spices.

All these were things that were scarce in the frontier settlements. Store boats floating down the river were often the only places to buy them. But the ladies did not always buy. They bargained and argued with the store-keeper if they thought his prices were too high.

Sometimes they just came to visit with each other and to look at the wares.

If the storekeeper did sell something, he might be paid with small bits of silver. In the early days on the Ohio River, Spanish dollars from New Orleans were often the only coins to be had. It was not easy to make change.

And so a dollar was sometimes cut like a pie into eight equal pieces called bits. To this day we often speak of a quarter of a dollar as "two bits."

Beyond the store boat, as likely as not, was an emigrant family's flatboat. Boys and girls probably scrambled about on its deck, laughing and playing. Their dog lay sleeping in the sun. A clothesline strung with washing flapped in the breeze. Mother sat on the deck, perhaps, mending clothes. Father may have been cleaning a mess of catfish he had caught for supper.

From still other boats came the mooing of cows, the grunting and squealing of pigs, and the cackling of chickens in a pen.

Most flatboatmen were friendly fellows. They liked to go from boat to boat, visiting each other. Sometimes they played cards or talked about the latest news on the river. There was almost sure to be one man who had a fiddle. Then they loved to have a dance on some flatboat's deck.

These jolly flatboatmen celebrate their arrival in a port with music and dancing. Painting by Bingham.

The women and older girls from the emigrant boats usually joined the dancing. But there seldom were enough of them to go around, so some of the men had to dance with each other. They danced lively, old-time country dances, clapping their hands to keep time with the fiddle. They stamped their feet and yelled and had a wonderful time.

But sooner or later, every flatboatman wanted to go ashore and see Shawneetown.

No one has left us a picture of old Shawnee-town. Like most early frontier towns, it probably was not very pretty. It had one main street, a wide, muddy lane that ran right along the riverbank. On one side was the great island of boats. On the other was a straggling row of buildings. Most of them were built of logs or of thick wooden slabs split from tree trunks with an ax. Very few were of stone or brick.

Many of these buildings were rough taverns where whiskey and rum were sold to the rivermen. Some were traders' stores. Sheds were used as warehouses. One slab building had a sign over the door: UNITED STATES LAND OFFICE. Here, emigrants who wanted to settle down in this region could buy land from the government.

Wagons pulled by ox teams rumbled up and down the muddy street. The drivers shouted and poked the oxen with poles to make them go. Some of the wagons were headed for a road that ran north to other settlements in Illinois. Several were bringing barrels of salt from salt springs not far from Shawneetown.

This activity helped to make the town a busy trading center. The salt would surely sell for high prices in other towns on the Ohio and Mississippi Rivers. So flatboatmen often bought a barrel or two to add to their cargoes.

The street was usually crowded with people. Dirty buckskin shirts and fur caps on some of the men showed that they were trappers and hunters. Sober brown homespun clothing on others showed them to be merchants, hurrying about town, eager to trade with the rivermen. Emigrants went in and out of the land office. Here and there was an Indian, wrapped in a tattered old blanket.

As evening came on, dim lamplight gleamed in the tavern windows. Snatches of song and loud, rough talk drifted out into the street.

50

Then, suddenly, a hush might fall. People in the street might glance nervously at one another. Everybody would turn to watch a group of men who came striding along from the river landing.

They were big fellows. They were dressed in bright flannel shirts, loose blue jackets, and skintight trousers of leather or linsey-woolsey. Some had round leather caps perched on their heads; some wore battered old cloth hats. A few had red turkey feathers stuck jauntily in their hats or caps.

The men looked pretty battered too. Several might have black patches covering one eye or the place where an eye had been. Some might be missing an ear. Their long hair hung down to their broad shoulders, and their beards were matted and shaggy.

They strutted along as if they owned the street. And the townfolk stepped aside and gave them plenty of room to pass. They had seen such men before.

They were keelboatmen.

This drawing of Mike Fink, a swaggering keelboatman,
appeared in *Davy Crockett's Almanack* in 1838.

6. Half Horse, Half Alligator

Keelboatmen liked to think that they were the kings of the river. And in some ways they were.

They sneered at flatboats, which only floated down the river. Keelboats traveled upstream as well as down. They carried valuable cargoes of cotton, sugar, rum, and other goods all the way up the Mississippi and the Ohio from New Orleans. No other boats could do it.

A keelboat was somewhat bigger than most flatboats. She was about 60 feet long or more, and quite narrow. She was named for the keel, a thick, strong timber which ran along the

whole length of her bottom. This protected the
boat from damage if it ran into a sunken log
or rock.

Like a flatboat, the keelboat was heavy and
strongly built, and needed only about two feet
of water to float. But with her sharp, curving
bow and stern and her rounded hull, she was
far more graceful than any flatboat.

Just the same, working a loaded keelboat
upstream against the swift, swirling river currents was a very hard job. And it was often
dangerous. It took a large crew, usually from
24 to 30 of the strongest, toughest fellows on
the river.

Keelboatmen were fiercely proud of that.

Once in a while, when the wind blew from

the right direction, they could rig a mast and sail that would drive the boat along. More often, they had to row her or push her upstream with long poles.

Down the center of the keelboat ran a high, narrow cabin where the cargo was stowed. On both sides of the cabin were open spaces called footways, which ran from the boat's bow clear to the stern. The captain sat up on the cabin roof and gave orders. The crew stood on the footways.

In all his travels, John James Audubon saw many a keelboat going up the river. In his journal he tells us how the crew worked:

"Two men, called bowsmen, remain at the prow to assist the steersman in managing the boat and keeping its head right against the current. The rest place themselves on the land side of the footway . . . put one end of their poles on the ground and the other end against their shoulders, and push with all their might. . . ."

As the boat moved ahead, each man walked slowly toward the stern, still pushing on his pole as hard as he could. At the stern he

lifted his pole, crossed to the other side of the boat, and ran up to the bow. Then he did the same thing all over again. The boat moved forward, wrote Audubon, at about one mile an hour.

It was slow going, and it went on for hour after hour. But in many places the water was too deep for the poles to reach bottom. And the current was often too strong for the boat to be rowed against it.

Then cordelling was the only thing to do.

A big thick rope, known as a cordelle, was attached to the boat. All the men except the captain and the steersman then jumped into the shallow water near the riverbank and towed her. That was the hardest work of all.

The men scrambled over logs and rocks and underbrush at the water's edge. They slipped and slithered through mud and sand. And they often had to do this, dragging the heavy boat behind them, for many miles at a stretch. Then, after a short rest, they went back to work with oars or poles.

No wonder keelboatmen were big and brawny. A weakling could never have stood the life they led.

It was no wonder, either, that when keelboatmen went ashore at a place like Shawneetown, they wanted to have some fun. But their idea of fun was pretty rough. Their arrival at a town, wrote Audubon, "was the certain forerunner of a riot."

Early travelers on the Ohio River told many tales of the keelboatmen. Perhaps their stories were not true. But their tales have become legends. So it is hard to say what these men really were like.

Keelboatmen certainly were fighters and

troublemakers. But we are told that all river-men—even the flatboatmen—were great boasters too. They loved to use big, bragging words when they talked about themselves.

A keelboatman might walk up to a husky flatboatman, jump high in the air, and crack his heels together. Then he might say something like this:

"Hey, look at me, friend! I'm half horse and half alligator, I am. I was raised by an old she-panther with a snapping turtle for my play-mate. I'm pure poison, and I can out-run, out-hop, out-jump, throw down, drag out, and lick any man in the country. So stand back and give me room!"

But the flatboatman, waving his fists and hopping around in a circle, might answer:

"See here, friend, I'm the man they call Sudden Death! I'm a rip-tailed roarer from the Salt River. I can eat a dozen rattlesnakes and drink a barrel of whiskey for my breakfast and I'm chock-full of fight. So bow your neck and hold your breath, lest I turn myself loose!"

So many such tales have been handed down to us that we must believe the rivermen really talked this way.

Sometimes the bragging became so loud and

violent that the men scared each other off. But when a fight broke out, it was sure to be wild and bloody.

These rivermen cared nothing about rules or good sportsmanship. They fought rough-and-tumble style, kicking and biting each other. Eyes might be gouged out, and ears torn off. The friends of the fighters usually got into the fight too. Then it was a furious free-for-all.

But at last the fun was over. The winners and losers staggered back to their boats. They patched each other up and lay down to sleep on the hard decks. Before sunrise it was time to work the boats again, in spite of their aches and pains.

Mooring lines were cast off. Through the chill of the gray morning, keelboat captains roared, "Stand to your poles!"

And then, a moment later, "Set off!"

The men leaned on their long poles. They began to walk down the footways. One by one, the keelboats moved up the river.

The flatboatmen cast off too. They rowed their clumsy craft out from the shore. Once more the current began to sweep them downstream. The dark, sleeping town fell behind. No doubt the flatboatmen were glad to see the last of Shawneetown and the keelboatmen for a while.

Rough as the keelboatmen were, however, they were not the worst men on the river. The flatboats would be lucky to escape trouble in the miles that lay ahead.

7. Some Rogues and Rascals

Below Shawneetown, shoals and islands dotted the river. The current flowed between the islands through narrow, crooked channels that were often choked with huge snags, rocks, and sandbars.

To make this stretch even worse, both the Illinois and Kentucky shores were wild and lonely.

In the olden days gangs of outlaws and river pirates lived there. Many of them were criminals who had been chased away from the settlements farther east. Some of them were the most evil men America has ever known.

Flatboatmen who fell into their hands were unlucky indeed.

One of the worst of the rascals called himself Colonel Plug.

We know little about the Colonel, for few of the travelers who met him ever lived to tell of it. His real name was said to be Fluger or Pfluger and he claimed that he had once been a soldier.

Soon after he came to the Ohio River, around 1800, Plug found a partner who went by the strange name of Nine-Eyes. We know even less about Nine-Eyes than we do about the Colonel. But the two men soon gathered a gang of other rascals about them. They became wreckers. Their plan was simple, and it worked nearly every time.

Colonel Plug pretended to be a river pilot. He liked to wait at some landing on shore until a flatboat came along and stopped there. Then he went up and got acquainted with the people on board. Finally, he offered to guide them through the dangerous shoals ahead.

Flatboatmen did sometimes hire pilots on bad sections of the river. And the Colonel must have been a very convincing fellow. Also he usually picked on unwary emigrants who were coming down the river for the first time. So he seldom had any trouble in fooling his victims.

Once the boat started down the river again, it was easy for him to steer it onto a rock or a snag. And of course, Nine-Eyes and the gang would be waiting nearby. If the poor flatboat folk were not drowned in the wreck, they were murdered in cold blood.

Then the wreckers fished the cargo out of the river and sold it at Shawneetown, or Red Bank, Kentucky, or some other small river town. In those days there was scarcely any law and order in the region. So nobody even bothered to ask where or how these fellows had gotten the goods.

For a long time, Colonel Plug was successful. But one day he tried a new trick, and that was a mistake.

This time, so the story goes, he sneaked on board a flatboat while its crew was looking the other way. He hid under the deck at the stern until they pushed off. Then he took out his knife and began to pick the oakum calking from between the planks in the bottom of the boat.

He thought that the boat would take a long

time to sink. So he had told his gang to wait some distance downstream. But it happened that this floatboat was very poorly built. The Colonel had barely begun to pick at the calking when the planks burst apart.

In rushed the water, trapping him under the deck. Down went the boat to the bottom of the river. And that was the end of Colonel Plug.

Plenty of other rogues were left, however.

About 20 miles down the river from Shawnee-town, a tall, rocky cliff jutted up on the Illinois shore. A large cave was there, high above the water. Some years before 1800, a man named Wilson opened a tavern in the cave. He put a sign down at the water's edge where the river-men could see it:

WILSON'S LIQUOR VAULT &

HOUSE FOR ENTERTAINMENT

After a while the place came to be called the Cave Inn. Later it was known simply as Cave-in Rock. Today, no one even remembers Wilson's first name. For all we know, he may have started out to be an honest innkeeper.

But Cave-in Rock became the worst den of outlaws on the whole Ohio River.

At first innocent folk who stopped to spend

A steamboat chugs peacefully past Cave-in Rock long
after the time that it was known as a den of thieves.

the night there were just murdered as they
slept. But soon the place had such an evil
reputation that no riverman would go ashore
at Cave-in Rock.

Then the outlaws began to go in skiffs to
attack passing boats. They were so bold, and
there were so many of them, that not even the
tough keelboatmen were safe from attack.

Sooner or later, over a period of several
years, every evil man in the whole region
joined the gang at Cave-in Rock. Two of the
most bloodthirsty were the Harpe brothers,
Micajah and Wiley.

Today we can understand that the Harpes

probably were a pair of insane men. Unlike most outlaws, they cared very little about money or the loot from a valuable flatboat. They were cruel, brutal fellows who simply enjoyed killing people.

Once while they were at the Rock, they helped to capture a flatboat with two emigrant families on board. Most of the people were murdered, as usual. But for some reason, one man was spared and taken prisoner.

That night the outlaws sat around a roaring fire near the mouth of the cave. They were singing and drinking while they divided the

emigrants' belongings. No one happened to notice that the prisoner had disappeared or that the Harpe brothers were not there either.

Then a terrible scream rang out from the top of the cliff.

There, high overhead, a horse and rider seemed to fly across the sky in the flickering light of the fire. But the rider was the unfortunate prisoner. The Harpes had taken him up to the top of the cliff and tied him to the horse's back. Then they drove the frightened beast over the edge.

While the outlaws gaped in amazement, the horse and rider plunged past them and were smashed to pieces on the rocks by the river, far below.

This was a bit too much for the rest of the outlaws. Wicked as they were, they were all disgusted by such senseless cruelty. They drove the Harpes away from the cave.

Not long afterward, Micajah was killed by a band of citizens in Kentucky. They cut off his head and nailed it to a tree. The place where the tree stood is known to this day as Harpe's Head. Wiley escaped for a while. But some years later he too was caught. He was hanged for his crimes.

The other outlaws stole from the rivermen for a long time. At last, though, word came that a fleet of flatboats was bringing soldiers down the river to attack the outlaws. When they heard that, they fled in all directions.

Still that was not the end of pirates on the river. For many more years other gangs went on robbing the flatboatmen whenever they had the chance. But Cave-in Rock, at least, became a safe place to stop.

When John James Audubon was there in 1820, he wrote that "this cave is one of the curiosities that attract the attention of almost every traveler on the Ohio, and thousands of names and dates ornament the sides and the ceiling."

After leaving Cave-in Rock, the flatboats still had to go through a very bad stretch of the river, known as the Hurricane Bars. But the men knew that now they were near the end of the Ohio.

In about a week, if all went well, they would be floating down the Mississippi.

8. The End of the Voyage

Even when they had reached the Mississippi, the flatboatmen still had a long way to go. It is more than a thousand miles from the mouth of the Ohio River to New Orleans. And the country ahead of the rivermen was as rough and wild as what lay behind them.

John James Audubon's journal gives us a hint of how rudely folk lived in the little settlement of New Madrid, Missouri, on the Mississippi River.

"They are clad in buckskin pantaloons and a sort of shirt of the same," he wrote. "This is seldom put aside unless it is so ragged or so blooded and greased that it will become disagreeable even to the poor wrecks that have it on."

The Mississippi is a great, broad river. It is generally brown and muddy, not like the clear, sparkling Ohio. It too was full of snags, sandbars, and other perils to the flatboatmen.

Passing the shores of Arkansas, for example, Audubon's boat came to the place where the White River flows out into the Mississippi. The White River was flooded at the time. Its waters poured out with such fury that the flatboat was tossed about by the waves and almost wrecked.

The crew had to run her ashore on the opposite bank of the Mississippi. It was plain that they would have to tow her for a way, as the keelboatmen did.

Evidently they didn't have enough rope. But flatboatmen were pretty good at making do with whatever they could find. They cut some wild grapevines on shore, twisted them together, and made what Audubon called "a natural cordelle." With this they dragged the flatboat about seven miles until it was safe to push out into the stream once more.

Gradually, the country changed as the river flowed south. The banks soon became low and marshy. The flatboatmen found themselves floating past great farms, called plantations,

Both oceangoing vessels and riverboats crowded the
busy harbor of New Orleans in flatboat days.

where cotton and sugar cane grew. The air
felt warm and balmy, although it was now
December.

Then one day the flatboat swung around a
bend in the river, and there was New Orleans.

In the year 1803, New Orleans had become
an American city. Long before that time the
Spanish had won it away from France in a
war. Then, in 1800, Spain agreed to give New
Orleans and the rest of the Louisiana Territory
back to France. But Americans had realized
that they did not want to have such an
important city owned by any foreign nation.

71

So President Thomas Jefferson bought New Orleans and all the Louisiana Territory for the United States. It made our nation more than twice as big as before. The price was about $15,000,000. Some people thought the President was foolish to pay so much, but it turned out to be a great bargain.

For a very long time afterward, New Orleans continued to be more like a foreign city than an American one.

Most of the people were called Creoles. They were descendants of French and Spanish settlers. They wore gay, bright-colored clothes. Their voices were soft and musical, and they used many French and Spanish words that the Americans did not understand. In fact, many different languages were heard in the streets of New Orleans.

People called immigrants, from Ireland, Germany, Italy, and other countries in Europe, had come across the sea to find new homes in America. A lot of them lived in New Orleans too.

Negro slaves walked about the streets. And the flatboatmen often met sailors from the ships that docked in New Orleans. Some of them wore big gold or brass rings in their ears,

The flag of France is lowered; the United States flag
is raised; and the Louisiana Territory joins our nation.

Crowds of people gathered on Sunday morning in the old French market of New Orleans to shop and gossip.

and had long mustaches. Almost everyone in the city seemed to be having a good time.

New Orleans was full of big houses, two or three stories high. The walls were covered with plaster that was tinted in soft shades of blue or yellow or pink. Many of the houses had beautiful courtyards where trees and flowers grew. Across the fronts of the houses ran long galleries, with railings of graceful ironwork.

Never had the rivermen seen such grand houses.

Along the streets were cafés and wineshops and markets with many kinds of fruit for sale.

From the cafés came the sounds of music and singing and pleasant smells of rich spices and roasting coffee.

All this seemed very strange and wonderful to the simple fellows from the Ohio River.

Yet they spent most of their time on the broad landing that ran along the river. In New Orleans, it was called the levee. This was where the flatboats were tied up. And this was where their cargoes were sold.

The busy season on the levee began in December, for that was when most of the flatboats arrived. To the rivermen it seemed at first like Shawneetown, but a hundred times

City folk enjoyed their Sunday afternoon stroll in New Orleans' Lafayette Park.

Flatboats have tied up at the levee to unload. The masts of sailing ships tower beyond.

busier. The lines of flatboats stretched for a mile or more along the river.

Beyond the flatboats tall masts and spars stuck up into the sky, as thickly as the trees in a great forest. These belonged to the big sailing ships that were moored there. They came from foreign ports all over the world. New Orleans was only a few miles from the Gulf of Mexico, and the ships could sail right up the river.

Some of the flatboat cargoes would be loaded on board these ships to be taken to foreign lands. But many other cargoes would be used by the people of New Orleans themselves.

The merchants of the city carried on their wholesale trade right there on the levee. If the flatboatmen were lucky, the goods they had brought might be scarce in New Orleans. Then they got high prices. If their goods were in plentiful supply, they might have to bargain hard in order to make a profit.

In the early days they were usually paid in Spanish money—either big gold doubloons or silver dollars. This went on for many years even after New Orleans had become an American city.

A flatboat often had to lie at the levee for several weeks before its cargo was all sold.

The cramped quarters of their flatboat were "home" for the crew until the last of their cargo was sold.

The men had no objections. They liked New Orleans and enjoyed some fine times there.

But finally the boat was empty. The last of the salt pork or shelled corn or whiskey or tobacco—or whatever else it had brought—was loaded into a wagon and hauled away. Then the flatboat was usually sold too.

New Orleans was a growing city. The good, sturdy wood in the flatboat could be used to build new houses. And besides, it would be almost impossible to row such a clumsy craft back up the river. So the poor old boat was hauled out of the water and broken up for lumber.

Now it was time for the men to start back home again.

9. The Long Walk Home

There were no bridges over the Mississippi River in those early days. And New Orleans lay on the west bank. So the voyagers had to start their trip home by hiring someone with a boat to take them across the river.

As soon as they stepped ashore on the east bank, the easy part of the trip was over.

If their flatboat cargo had happened to bring good prices, they might buy horses or mules to ride. But more often they just slung their blanket rolls over their shoulders and started walking home.

The road ran northward for about a hundred miles, through gloomy swamps beside the river. Then the travelers came to the small town of Natchez, Mississippi. They might stay overnight at an inn there. That would be their last chance to sleep in a real bed or eat a good meal, for many a day.

The road out of Natchez was called the Natchez Trace. It turned away from the river and ran northeast for over five hundred miles. And every step of that long way was wilderness land that still belonged to the Choctaw and Chickasaw Indians.

Natchez, overlooking the Mississippi River, was the first stop on the long trip home.

The Natchez Trace was a rude trail, rather than a road. It was so narrow and so cluttered with tree stumps that wagons could not even pass over it. Huge, gnarled trees and dense thickets, or canebrakes, pressed in on both sides. At night travelers had to camp wherever they could. They might go for days without seeing a house of any kind.

Most of the Indians were friendly. But gangs of white bandits might be lurking anywhere along the Trace. Many of these wretches roamed this wild country. They were every bit as bad as the pirates of Cave-in Rock.

The flatboatmen usually protected themselves by traveling in parties of a dozen or more. They hid the coins they had received at New Orleans by sewing them inside their shirts or trousers. Still they often ran into trouble.

An old story has been handed down to us from the early 1800's. It tells about a party of flatboatmen who were camped one night at a place called Gum Springs. They built a roaring fire and cooked and ate their supper. Then they got ready to go to sleep.

One of them, looking for a place to spread out his blanket, wandered away from the fire. He stumbled over a bandit lying in the brush.

Up jumped the bandit, yelling and firing his gun. In an instant a whole gang of bandits came rushing out of the dark forest, yelling and shooting their guns too. The flatboatmen, frightened out of their wits, ran away as fast as they could go.

Luckily, none of them had been hurt. But they hid in the woods all night long, shivering and quaking.

Early the next morning a man named John Swaney came riding by on his horse. Swaney was a postman. It was his job to carry the United States mail over the Natchez Trace. When he found the deserted camp, he blew a blast on his bugle. After a while the flatboatmen began to straggle out of the woods.

They were a sad sight. Many had left their clothes behind when they ran off. Their leader, a big, hulking fellow from Kentucky, had nothing on but his shirt. But when they saw that the bandits were gone, they grew very brave all of a sudden.

They decided to chase the bandits and get back their property. All their guns, as well as their money and clothes, had been stolen. So they snatched up sticks and stones for weapons and set out after the bandits. Since the bandits

had not bothered to hide their trail, it was easy to follow.

Striding along ahead of the rest was the big man from Kentucky with his shirttails flapping about his legs. He roared and shouted, telling of the terrible things he was going to do to the bandits when he caught them.

Then he found his trousers lying on the ground.

Glory be! All his coins—four gold doubloons—were still sewed inside the waistband. Somehow the robbers had overlooked the money when they dropped the trousers.

Almost at once, Mr. Swaney, the postman, noticed that the big fellow stopped his blustering. Instead of leading the chase, he began lagging in the rear. And just then everyone was startled by a gruff voice from a thicket ahead, saying, "Clear out, or we'll kill every last one of ye!"

The bandits were waiting there, crouched behind trees with their guns ready.

Many years later when he wrote this story, John Swaney ended by remarking, "The big Kentuckian outdistanced the whole party in the race back to camp."

Most of the flatboatmen never did get back their money or their clothes. But they were lucky, all the same. As often as not, the bandits of the Natchez Trace not only robbed their victims but murdered them as well.

The Natchez Trace ended at Nashville, Tennessee. From there on, returning flatboatmen took the old Wilderness Road that led up into Kentucky. They still had a long, wearisome walk ahead of them. But the country was settled now, with houses and farms along the way.

And soon the party would begin to split up when each man headed for his own home in Kentucky or Ohio or Indiana.

So at last, one by one, their journeys ended.

We can imagine how joyfully a flatboatman's family must have greeted him when he strode up to the cabin door. Perhaps they did not always recognize him immediately, for he may have looked like a stranger.

He was probably dirty and burned brown by the wind and sun. His clothes were in tatters, his boots broken and cracked from the long walk home. His hair was long and tangled. Quite likely, he had let his beard grow.

But the old dog would surely bark and wag his tail frantically. Younger brothers and sisters would come running with whoops of joy.

Mother undoubtedly had to wipe away a tear of happiness. And Father would be very proud of his strapping son.

The money from New Orleans would be welcome too. For many a poor family, it might be almost all the cash income they would have for the whole year.

Today we would think flatboating a pretty hard way to earn a living.

But most flatboatmen were ready to make another trip the following year. Some, like "Walking" Wilson of Maysville, Kentucky, made more than one trip a year. We may not know a great deal about Mr. Wilson, but he certainly earned his nickname.

During the years from 1803 to 1824, he made 33 voyages to New Orleans. He walked back 20 times, a total of 16,000 miles. Twelve times, he came back on horseback. On his last trip he rode a steamboat home.

That was a sign of changing times.

10. The Last Flatboats

A strange-looking craft started down the Ohio River from Pittsburgh one day in 1811. Her name was the *New Orleans*, and she was the first steamboat ever seen on the river. Her voyage was the beginning of a new era.

By the early 1820's, many other steamboats were chugging up and down the Ohio and the Mississippi.

They soon put the keelboats out of business. A steamboat was bigger than any keelboat. Her huffing, puffing engines and her churning paddle wheels made her go much faster. After a while, no one wanted to ship goods by the old keelboats any more.

Some of the tough, brawling keelboatmen went off to the wild country west of the Mississippi. Out there, on great rivers like the Missouri, there were not many steamboats yet. What happened to most of them after that? They simply disappeared.

But steamboats didn't bother flatboatmen a bit. The farmers who lived along the Ohio River were thrifty folk. And they were seldom in a hurry. They saw no reason for hiring some

Rivermen on the wild Missouri River faced dangerous Indian attacks as well as tricky currents.

newfangled steamboat to take their crops to market for them. So the flatboats went right on floating down the broad Ohio just as they had before.

One thing was changed, however. Like "Walking" Wilson, all flatboatmen began to ride home on the steamboats. It was easier than walking, and the fare was cheap. Usually deck passage on a steamboat only cost from $3.00 to $6.00.

Before long, hardly anyone traveled over the old Natchez Trace.

As the years passed, the states along the Ohio became settled and prosperous. More and more emigrants moved there. Cities like Louisville and Cincinnati grew great and bustling. Fine, fertile farms replaced the forests along all of the rivers that flowed into the Ohio.

And all this made the river commerce grow.

By the 1840's, records showed that there were about 450 steamboats on the Ohio. But there were more than 4,000 flatboats.

Some of them were much bigger than the old arks, broadhorns, and Allegheny skiffs. But many still were small craft with families living on board. These folk fished in the river and traded with people in the river towns.

In the year 1861, war broke out between the states of the North and the states of the South. Fierce fighting along the Mississippi put a stop to flatboating for a while. Some of the flatboatmen went off to fight in the war. Some stayed home to tend their farms.

When the war ended in 1865, they went back to flatboating once again. But now great changes were on the way.

One of the last of the flatboatmen was Captain William Devol. He lived on a farm near Marietta, Ohio. His ancestors had been rivermen for many years.

Flatboatmen and raftsmen soon found that they were sharing frontier rivers with "newfangled steamboats."

William Devol started out on his last flatboat trip in the fall of 1872. He had built his own boat, which was nearly 100 feet long. It held 1,000 barrels packed with salt pork, apples, and potatoes. This cargo was worth about $6,000.

The boat had a snug cabin about six feet wide, with an iron stove, a folding table, and a bed. So we can see that Captain Devol was more comfortable than John James Audubon and his companions had been, back in 1820. Still Devol didn't have a very easy time of it.

When he started out, he was also in charge of several flatboats that belonged to his neighbors. Hoping to have a speedy trip, he hired a steamboat to tow this string of boats down the river.

What a change from the old days that was! Now flatboats were often towed by steamboats.

At Louisville, Kentucky, the weather turned cold. The river froze, trapping the boats in thick ice. And there they stayed for five weeks. All day and all night the flatboat crews kept hot fires burning in their stoves to keep the potatoes and apples from being frozen.

At last the ice broke up and let the boats go free. But big chunks of ice still clogged the river. The steamboat made slow time as it

towed the flatboats along. Even the Mississippi
was full of drifting ice.

Seventy-one days after setting out from home,
William Devol finally reached Memphis, Tennessee. He decided that flatboating had become
more trouble than it was worth. So he was
glad when a chance came to sell his cargoes
in Memphis. Then he got on a railroad train
and went home.

That was another sign of change. By 1872, railroads had been built all over America. The trains could carry all the goods that people used or needed.

William Devol never made another flatboat trip. Before long, other men stopped making them too.

Nearly a hundred years had passed since brave Parson Tucker had fought the Indians and died a hero. In that time flatboating had become a way of life for thousands of pioneer folk in the Ohio Valley. And the flatboatmen had helped to push the frontier westward.

But old ways were out of date now. America was growing into a mighty, fast-moving nation. Smart young fellows no longer wanted to go flatboating.

The old, adventurous days on the Ohio River were gone forever.

Glossary

adz: a tool with a curved blade that is used to smooth wood

Allegheny skiff: a flatboat that has a large, flat-roofed house on its deck

ark: a big, awkward boat with a pointed bow and stern

bateau: a large skiff

broadhorn: another name for a Kentucky boat

budget: a bag or pouch in which rivermen carried their personal possessions

calico: a bright-colored cotton cloth, most usually printed in a pattern

calking: the filling packed in the seams of wooden boats to make them watertight

canebrakes: a dense growth of sugarcane plants

cordelle: a heavy rope used for towing keelboats

Creoles: people descended from French or Spanish settlers of Louisiana

doubloon: an old Spanish coin that was made of gold

emigrants: people who leave one region or country to settle in another

gallery: a balcony

gouge oars: large oars used to row flatboats

homespun: a kind of cloth made of yarn spun at home

immigrant: a person who comes into a foreign country to make his home

keelboat: a narrow riverboat that could be poled upriver

Kentucky boat: the most common kind of flatboat. It had a low slanting roof that covered most of its length

levee: a dock or landing place for vessels of all kinds

linsey-woolsey: a rough homespun cloth made of wool mixed with linen or cotton

mast: an upright pole supporting the sails of a ship

oakum: strands of tarred rope used as calking

pirogue: a canoe made by hollowing out the trunk of a tree

powder horn: a container made of an animal's horn, used to carry gunpowder

ramrod: a metal rod for ramming a charge of gunpowder down the muzzle of the gun

scow: a large flat-bottomed boat with square ends, used to carry cargo

skiff: a light rowboat

spar: a ship's mast

tallow: the hard fat of cows and sheep which is melted for use in candles and soap

Index